LIE'F

LIE'F

Luis Martinez

XULON PRESS

Xulon Press
2301 Lucien Way #415
Maitland, FL 32751
407.339.4217
www.xulonpress.com

Printed in the United States of America.

ISBN-13: 9781545636305

Table of Contents

Introduction

*T*hroughout my years of working with people who need some type of guidance or advice, I've realized that it helps to give it to them in a way that they will understand. I have dealt with many knuckleheads in my lifetime. I have tried many different ways to get my point across to them: suit-and-tie conversations, counselor-to-client exchanges, and even stooping to their level to have an effective chat. Nevertheless, nothing seemed to work better than talking to them exactly how they talked because they could relate to that better. Sometimes you have to speak to people in their own language—you just can't meow to a lion or lizard your way to gator.

Those who hang out on the streets don't want to hear an educated conversation. They don't want to hear advice, and most of them don't think that they are doing anything wrong (regardless of legality). Most will tell you that if someone wants to get high, it should be okay to sell the drug to them. It's their life, they argue, and if they want to waste it, they should be able to do so. In some ways, that position makes a lot of sense. One thing that they leave out, however, is that, along with what they are doing, comes a lot of violence and deaths. But drug dealing isn't the only thing that creates violence these days—politics and religion are up there, too. At the end of the day, it's all about money, power, and respect.

In this book, I decided to write what entered my mind and express it exactly that way. Some may like it, others may feel it's a little offensive, but what is life if we can't express how we really feel about it and the issues we deal with daily. Sometimes we need to say what many people only think. Sometimes we need to hear things to realize just how stupid or ridiculous our lifestyles have become. Some people go an entire lifetime without someone stopping them to let them know that they are doing things wrong or that they need change in their lives. What would you rather deal with: the truth that hurts, or liars who are afraid of offending you?

In this book, though, I'm improving on the first option. You don't have to *hear* people saying harshing words, you can *read* this book and get something out of it to help you change some of your ways. As I wrote this book, I realized that I was guilty in some ways, too. After all, I grew up in denial. People say negativity is what sells; I say people would rather listen to what's more interesting. When everything is okay, people read magazines; when times get rough, they're quick to pick up a Bible.

By the way, I already know the response I'm going to get from this book. Criticizing me isn't going to make the world a better place. Instead, you have to have fun in life while you are still breathing. This is my way of doing that. Enjoy.

Chapter 1

Let It Go

*A*ll I've ever wanted in my life was to be comfortable with knowing that I had done everything possible to be happy. Sometimes I feel like I have done more than I have received, but I have learned many lessons from all my losses. That's what my life has been about: I set my expectations so high that when I come up short, I feel like I have failed. It took me years to understand, but I have probably learned a lot more from failure than from success. Someone does have to lose. If you understand that, you'll figure out that mostly everything in life is a fifty-fifty shot, even when you are challenging yourself. Mentally, you will challenge what you try to do physically and, many times, you'll end up emotionally drained. This manifests in many different ways. It can be seen in the people you deal with daily, the goals you set that never go according to plan, and the way luck plays out.

People see me every day and think that nothing in my life seems to bother me or that my life is as perfect as they can imagine. But what they can't see are my thoughts, or the nightmares I have to deal with almost every night. I've had so many anxiety attacks that I often feel like I'm taking my last breath. No one is there when I'm alone in my room, just wishing and praying that things in my life could be different. No one is there when I'm reminiscing about things I could have done differently. I have wished for death for so long that I feel like I'm being punished to live. My mom told me one day that, because I have faced death so many times and nothing has ever happened to me, I'm going to live to see a hundred years. I hope not. Although life is too short to be sitting around complaining all the time, it is too damn long when you're struggling. People have told me that I just need to go to church and pray. Listen, I'm going to need Jesus at night when I'm sleeping, plus one disciple per hour to get me through my hardest days.

Ever since I was a kid, I always pictured a perfect life. As an adult, I've been dreaming with my eyes open—constantly wishing and regretting. My problem is that I think I have allowed too many things to pile up in my life and can't seem to break away from them. It has always been easy to hear people tell me to get over things that I can't change. I have allowed all of these things that I can't change to control my life. One thing that really bothers me today, is knowing that, when I was young I had it made. I had the friends, I had the attention, and I had the popularity. It was a rush I wish I could wake up to all over again. It wasn't enough just having this kind of attention as an athlete, though. I also wanted things in life in a way that most teens these days literally die for. My biggest regret was thinking that my life was forever going to be like that of a teenager. But look how quickly it all just ends and seems to disappear. These days, I live everyday like it's my last. I'm not saying I'll just do anything; I don't want to have to look back and wish I would have done things I may not be able to do later.

When you're young, it seems like you have a lifetime to make up for what you could have done yesterday. Now that I am older, I wish I could just go back and erase mostly everything (and everybody) I thought was the greatest thing ever. What sucks about life is that, mentally, you have a picture of what you would like your life to be like, but doing it seems almost impossible. That's one of my biggest issues. I have failed so much that I don't even want to try anymore at times. I guess you can say that failing has made me a little insecure. Even today, people tell me that I need to do something with myself. They see potential that I no longer have the motivation to pursue. In a lot of ways, I fear rejection—and that's without even trying to pursue a goal. Deep inside, I want to do something in my life that I can one day look back on and be proud of. Even something small would suffice.

I've come to the understanding that, if I want things to change for the better, I shouldn't continue to punish myself for things I can't change. Nevertheless, one important thing I have accepted is that I don't need anyone. The fewer people I have to deal with, the better. I have learned that, once you meet someone or have too many people in your circle, you inherit their problems as well. Everything they deal with, you may have to suffer from, too. These days, it seems like everyone has problems. One or two friends is good enough.

You know what else I began not caring about? Money! I feel like I have been broke my entire life. Nevertheless, when it comes time to do whatever I consider fun, I spend whatever I have to enjoy the moment. I might as well enjoy what I can't take with me; you never know when it's time to go.

In this world, only an inmate would probably want to trade places with me. Anyone else would balk at my daily issues. Although they are all mental, they continue to limit me physically in terms of motivation to escape my past. I've taken the good with the bad, and I have compared my life to others who are doing worse. The best thing that I have ever done was not slip through the cracks. One thing I fear is that, eventually, something worse than what I am going through will happen, allowing me to see that my life is not all that bad. Yes, I have some issues, but I have seen and heard of a lot worse. In this book, I will give to you many examples of these hardships. Some may be a little over the top or offensive, but I'm sure many of you have also experienced comparable things.

On that note, here is the reason I decided to write this book: I wanted everyone to be able to read my thoughts— thoughts that others may think of but are afraid to express. I have always written about my opinions and I have decided to let all of my personal thoughts out in this book. I guess you could call it a stress reliever. I've needed to do this for a very long time. Who knows, maybe it will finally make me feel a lot better. The title of this book — *Lie'f* — is a little different. It pretty much describes what I believe most of us are going through in this world. Through it all, I honestly feel that we are all just living a lie. Most of us are being misled daily through promises by others who are simply just trying to benefit from us in every way possible. The more we allow it, the more we will continue struggle. We can blame and point the finger at others forever by putting all of our trust in them, but in the end, we are the stupid ones that continue to believe and fall for it. These are all of the things that I have always thought needed to come to light. Like I said, it may get a little personal, but it will also be very honest and to the point. I will write about some of the people in my life; I will share my thoughts on politics, religion, sex, and even some of my biggest secrets.

Chapter 2

Saying What Others Won't

*I*f you haven't already noticed, this world is coming down to the point where no one really gives a fuck about things that used to mean something. For example, do you really think that anyone cares about who is going to be the next president of the United States of America? Why should we? Why the fuck should anyone care about someone who doesn't care about us? We live in the most violent and drug infested country in the world that is making millions by the day from our downfalls. Nothing on this planet compares to what we are going through here in America. But although we expect so much from the leadership of this country, they are not to blame entirely for the escalating crime rate and all the drug addicts who are overdosing by the hundreds every night.

You know what else has become less important to people these days?

Being a responsible parent.

Who is giving birth to children with people they are actually planning a future with anymore? If a chick is easy enough to fuck after being at the club dancing all night, she can easily become someone's baby mother. You know, I say this and it offends all the right people. And you know who that is: the chicks who are out dancing getting drunk every weekend and getting pregnant by guys they just met who are so into the pussy that they forget to pull out (and then they sober up and the first thing that they say is, "It ain't mine"). That's the reason why this country is so fucked up. I don't know the percentage of kids who grow up without a father, but I bet if they studied how well the parents knew each other before they fucked, the results would be pretty embarrassing. When they realize they messed up, all they care about is child support. How about supporting your child by making him or her with a responsible father you didn't meet a half an hour ago and fucked before finding out his last name? And why are parents still dressing better than their kids? Why are they still in the club drunk at the age of thirty-five with five kids by deadbeat dads who all know each other?

Why are people still standing on a corner like it's not obvious what they are doing?

Drug dealers standing on a corner
as obvious as prostitutes.

I know I was guilty of doing so at one point in my life, but why are people who have been caught five or six times still acting like no one knows exactly what they are doing? Let me give you a hint, if you are over twenty-five and never had a job, chances are you'll never be able to find an employer who will pay you more than minimum wage. It sucks, but it's true. I have one thing to say to a drug dealer: one day, really soon, you're going to look back and say, where the hell did all my money and time go? As a matter of fact, stop right now and answer that question. I can almost guarantee you that you were doing a lot better before you started selling drugs. What's worse is that, if you haven't been caught, it hurts a lot more when you've had a longer run. In the end, you'll lose everything overnight. Want to know how? It's simple: the older you get, the less you want to go to jail. You will give up everything, including the people you dealt with, to avoid going to prison. Ever wonder why certain people's bonds are stronger than others? Judges, cops, bail bondsmen, and lawyers—they're not stupid. The more you sell, the more they assume you've got stashed away.

I hope that, in the end, you have enough to get out *and* stay out. Because these days, they aren't just trying to keep everyone in, they are trying to kill you as well.

It's fucked up, but when they say that the truth hurts, it only hurts the people who are actually doing the things you are reading about. If you don't have an education, a father figure, or a high-paying job, you're pretty much fucked. Times are getting harder and harder every day. These days, you need a part-time job for gas to make it to your full-time job to pay for the bills. And if you think that the government cares about you struggling, well, it's half your fault anyway. If you would have been trying to get an education, build a good enough resume, or keep yourself out of prison, you wouldn't be in the situation that you are in now. Yes, it is fucked up to hear or read about stuff like this, but it's more fucked up when a child has a different step-father every other weekend. If you ask most men why he left his so-called baby mama, it could be one of many things. The most important one of them all is because his intentions weren't to be in a relationship in the first place. It's a sad excuse to leave the mother of your children, but it happens.

You know, another thing that sucks to have to hear about is when someone is living wretchedly but blames everyone but themselves. And then they tell you that the reason for living that way is because it's all they know how to do. You mean to tell me that all you know how to do is wake up and do the same shit every day? Is it not obvious to you that when you see people waking up every morning to go to work that maybe—just maybe—you could be doing the same thing? It doesn't scare you that one day your record is going to be so fucked up that being in prison may be the best choice for you? I'm scared for you. I would hate to drive by people and say, "You see that guy right there? He was the best athlete in our state. You see that woman right there? She was the best-looking girl back in the day." It sucks when you fall into that category. Shit, it sucks for me because I could have been a great athlete myself; I know how tough it can be to be labeled a *Loser*.

If not having a father in your life is the reason you decided to make mistakes, that is no different than saying,

"Like father like son." If that doesn't make any sense to you, I don't know how else to put it into words. I mean, how are you comfortable becoming something that you blamed all of your life for? Here it is in other words: I hate the father I never met (or was never around), but I'm going to grow up to be just like him by finding a chick who is going to give me some ass on the first night, get her pregnant, and then leave her so the kid can be punished like I was. Like D. L. Hughley said, "We have enough daddies, but not enough fathers." Because the only time fathers seem to want to step up is when their baby mamas move on to fuck someone else.

Here's another issue: people struggling who didn't even get past high school (by choice) but are sitting collecting comfortably while section eight pays for everything. What kind of sense does that make? Shit, I wish I could just sit back and collect. I'll even make the government proud of me. I'll collect and bust my ass with a full- and part-time job. I think that's a better deal than just giving the money away. And why am I being drug tested to keep my job? Why aren't these people who are collecting and buying crack or heroin with free unearned money getting drug tested? They are the ones who are fucking up our neighborhoods. Or is it just a way for the system to keep people down? You know what, that's not even a good enough excuse. I know that there are some people who do need help, but there are many more that are lazy and just don't give a fuck.

I say put all of that free money into budgets for the people who actually work and raise the minimum wage for those who are trying. This way, I feel like we're helping instead of losing hard-earned money that ends up in a drug dealer's hands anyways. Now that I think about it, it is the middle class who always ends up getting fucked. Think about it: if you are rich, people give you shit for free; if you are poor by choice, all you have to do is get in line along with others who dropped out or can't find a hard-working partner while you sit back and gossip all day about other people. The middle class, the ones who actually do all the work, get screwed. Can you see how all these things are connected?

It sucks when we voice our opinions but get criticized for being too rough; yet, if a kid gets shot or stabbed while coming home from school, we want to lock up all the per-petrators. It's not until it hits home that people actually start paying attention. As for me, I have been on both sides.

What's sad is that I can't win. Sometimes—and it's only a thought—I feel like I have to go back to the streets just to make a little more money to pay my bills. Maybe I need to find a chick on section 8 who claims other people's kids on their taxes and triples their refund so I can live comfortably forever after. Just a joke—I'd rather not. I can't just sit back playing a PlayStation, smoking twenty blunts a day, laughing at nothing, and going grocery shopping twice a week because I have to feed six kids that are not mine.

How long do you think it is going to take for people to figure out that 99 percent of every money-making opportunity that people promise is a scam? Everything including casinos, lottery tickets, medication, illegal drugs, and prisons are money-making businesses. Don't get me wrong, if you do illegal things, you deserve to be locked up, but it is a business. Everything is about money. If it isn't, it's not important. You really shouldn't believe that a pill is going to erase your pain; the pills only hide pain. The illegal drugs in the streets come from the ones who are supposed to keep them out of the country. How many people do you know who have won the lotto? Why do you think casinos make so much money? It's obvious that everybody can't be a winner. They reach a certain amount for the month: one or two lucky people in the entire building will hit the jackpot. Most of us are stupidly inclined to get a quick fix and a fast dollar.

One thing that makes me question those who preach the good word are those pimp pastor-preachers. I know a lot of people have seen it themselves. Think about this: why is a pastor who preaches to people who pray for a miracle every day driving a Range Rover, a BMW, or a Mercedes? Why is that person living in a big-ass house and sporting a Rolex? Shit, at least play it off a little bit. Here I am getting yelled at by my supervisor for eating my lunch in front of a starving inmate who's eating shitty food, and these preachers are living like kings from people's donations. They say you can enter a church as you please. I think a preacher goes to church to try to please in a whole different way. Of course, it is also a business. I bet if Jesus himself walked right into their church they would be the first ones to say He's an imposter. Most of them just prey on the weak.

Here's my opinion: this country is rotting from the inside out. This country, although it may temporarily look like the best country to live in, is really not looking good in terms of the future. My prediction is that this country will continue to get worse because of all the excuses the government is coming up with. For example, these gas prices. It's all a joke—oil shortage? Damn, from one year to the next? And on top of that, we're in the Middle East stealing it? It reminds me of how cheap cocaine was until they killed Escobar. All of a sudden, the prices went up. The drug war brought the prices up because there was more to buy once it was brought into the country. Now gas is more expensive because there is more being brought in. I wish that the entire country would just get together for one whole week and just not pump any gas. Don't be surprised if one day that this country takes over all bank accounts and leaves everyone starving just to pay off debts or to help out other countries. That's probably why every-thing is done with credit cards these days. Imagine if they just shut the doors to every bank. What then? All you are left with is a plastic card worth nothing.

So what do you think so far? I'm going to try to voice my opinion on every single topic that I can think of in order to somehow how figure out how we ended up in this situation. I'm going to find the most honest way to say it without caring about how I say it. Because these are things that people want to say, but don't. It's like they say, many claim to want to know the truth, but they don't want to hear it. Damn, if I knew that all I had to do was nothing all of my life so that the system would feel sorry for me, I would have blown it off from the start. Not really—I'm just saying. Please, try not to get offended. Just laugh about it if it hits home. Have fun while reading. By the way, it's nothing personal.

Chapter 3

Hustler

I know I'm going to catch a lot of heat from those I stood next to selling crack and drinking beer with all day, but fuck it: I'm sure they understand. It's not like I'm snitching or anything like that. I'm just writing about my experiences and opinions about this dream we all shared of becoming big-time drug dealers who were going to be living in big houses and driving expensive cars. Unfortunately, most pretty much just ended up dead, in and out of prison and living house to house with relatives or friends who still cared about them. Honestly, if I took the time to share my thoughts with anyone who is still living the life of crime, I would simply tell them to just give it up. Of course, you're going to have the two or three lucky ones who are just getting by tell me that *I'm "hatin"* on them because I have to work for my money, but it's all funny to me.

Like I have said, I have been on both sides of the game. I have been a drug dealer and seen many drug dealers beg for an extra minute on the phone with a chick that's probably half-dressed to go out to a club with the new dude who took over. You have to remember that most men still have a little kid inside of them. On the outside, money gives them power, but on the inside, it's completely the opposite. That's where all of the pain is hidden. I know because I have been there. I have dealt with it personally, and I have seen even the toughest guys break down and cry. I have to admit, it is kind of funny—not that they cry, but because I remember how tough they were when their pants were sagging over their ass, and now they have creased their pants because they found religion in a cell. Then they lose it when they get released. Is it me, or is their God locked up? No one seems to find Him unless they end up in prison.

A few facts about a drug dealer: a drug dealer is one who stands on a corner, probably never had a job, has two or three kids, drinks liquor or smokes weed (or maybe even crack) every day, and will most likely snitch. All you have to do is scare the guy enough to think that someone else is going to end up with his girl when he gets locked up, and he'll tell you things cops never even thought about investigating. And yes, like many others who claimed they never would, most end up using the same shit they once sold. They call it curiosity; I call them drug addicts—exactly what they are. If it was up to them, they would deny everything even after they came out of rehab. These days, it's hard to really know who is selling drugs or smoking it. The dealer and the user both look like they are fucked up these days. It looks like it's no longer about looking good because they look like exactly what they claim the game is: a big struggle.

Growing up, I used to think that it was cool to stand on a corner all day selling drugs and running from a shootout. Nothing was fun unless it was crazy or violent enough to talk about all week. People got caught with drugs on them, shot, stabbed, and killed. But do you think that anything would stop anyone from thinking twice about going right back to the same spot? You're crazy if you think that. The only thing that would stop a person from selling drugs is a cell, and that's only temporary. And the other, I suppose, is death. The illusion of getting rich from selling drugs is similar to an addicted gambler. Here's the part that may confuse you a bit, though. Let's just say, for example, that you just made a hundred dollars. Do you know where at least sixty of it is going? Let me help you out a bit. It's either going to liquor, weed, or sneakers. And then they wonder why they call it a struggle. It wouldn't be much of a struggle if they did the obvious. How about saving some of the money instead of showing it off? I'm not giving advice to drug dealers; I'm only speaking about the ones who are actually out there trying to make a career out of it.

I have seen people get shot, come out of the hospital, and go right back to the same corner to sell drugs all over again. I don't know whether it's to show off and say, "They tried to kill me, but I'm still here," or if it's, "I'm here for a reason". I can almost guarantee one or two things that are going to happen: they will either get shot again or, in fear of getting shot, will shoot the first thing that scares them. But as stupid as most of them are, they'll probably get caught with the gun first. Why? They will probably be too high to realize that, though they were making a deal, the cops were right behind them. I don't care how slick, how smart, or how good you are, you will get caught eventually. And if you have already been caught, don't you think it would be that much easier to catch you again each and every time you decide to stand on the same spot you got caught on before? It does not make any sense. It's like they walk around with an "arrest me" sign on the back of their shirts.

I will be honest—this is as honest as I will get about selling drugs—the only way that I will go back is if I'd never get caught, never get shot, and never be betrayed. *In other words, never.* Now why is it that if I can think like that, others can't see it that way? I don't care if I can't pay my bills on time. Nothing is going to make me go back to getting snitched on or shot at because the collection agency keeps calling me. Nothing is that serious for me to throw it all away. Not a day goes by in which a snitch can't find a new person to tell on. Things will never be how they used to be. These days, it's all about being tough and flashy. Most go from tough stares to facing life in a cell... or dead in a coffin.

But why the tough stares and intimidating looks? They should save all of that to intimidate the cellmates who may try to fuck them up over their bottom bunk or Ramen noodles. No one in society really cares that a dealer sells drugs to earn illegal money; they wish they would just kill each other. But other than that, they don't care. You know why? Because they know that a dealer is out there on borrowed time. They are all just a temporary problem. *Because if the cops don't get to them first, someone who doesn't like them will.* It's sad to say, but these dealers these days are not only younger and stupider, but also disrespectful and a lot more violent. That's why they don't fight. They are all scared of each other so they'd rather just kill and end up being somebody's bitch in prison, crying for a low bail because they can't survive in a cell.

These days, everything is out in the open. I mean, why not just find a job so they can at least explain to a judge that they were trying? Surveillance is a real thing. Investigations are real, too. Don't think that just because they didn't come and get you yesterday or today that they won't be there tomorrow. You're not that good just because you did a hand-to-hand exchange in a car and the cops didn't catch you. The one who bought the drugs was probably an undercover officer. Did he look like he did drugs? Did he look like a drug addict? Just because he bought from you more than once, it does not mean that he's a real user.

I know what it feels like to have someone in your face trying to help you change. Believe me, I know how aggravating it can be. Maybe you should try listening like most of us should have. You would probably have better luck bungee jumping a thousand times off bridge and making it versus standing on a corner a second too long. But trying to have a conversation with a drug dealer is like listening to a rapper on a song: no matter what they say, they always contradict themselves. Face it: the streets don't choose anyone to become a drug dealer; people become what they want to become. You can't blame it on bad luck. Don't blame it on the environment. And please don't blame an entire society. I was out there myself. Shit, most of my family was. But we all got out. Some got shot, some ended up in prison, some got snitched on, and some had kids they probably regret. But the point is that, if you can, you should try to find a new and better way to make a living. That street shit isn't going to last forever.

Understand this: there is more to a future than Friday and Saturday nights. You can't just sit on your ass all day just to look forward to a weekend and the first or fifteenth of every month. Been there and done that. I'm not trying to tell you that it wasn't fun. As a matter of fact, try it out for yourself. A few years later, you'll be saying the same shit I'm saying. See, I made it out. I'm just trying to tell you that you might not. Life is really fucking short to be wasting it all in the streets trying to make money. Life is a lot longer when you are struggling in a cell crying all day. Everyday feels like hell when you have nothing in life. In a cell, every second, every minute, every hour, every day, every month, and every year will be about reminiscing about what you used to have or wondering what life could have been like had you chosen a different path. I mean, seriously, how can anyone be sad after seeing their friends being sent to prison forever or after watching a coffin with their friend in it going down slowly, but then end up the falling the same way?

It was being a drug dealer that started all these dreams and fantasies of making enough money to live comfortably. What a fucking joke that was. All dealing drugs did for me was sell me a dream. The only thing I am happy about my drug dealing past is that I didn't get shot dead or end up in prison. I want to make this clear to all of the people who are out there selling drugs today—and please understand this—there is going to be that one day where you are going to be sitting in a cell constantly saying to yourself that you should have stopped yesterday. And what may be worse about that day is that you may not be in for selling drugs ... You'll be in for murder. All for saving a person you probably would have never met had you not gone down that route in life.

Only real soldiers should put their lives in the hands of another. And by real, I don't mean what drug dealers and criminals call *keeping it real*. Out of all the horrible things that could happen, you'll likely survive getting shot. And I know that getting shot won't stop certain people from continuing the same path. These people think that there is a reason they didn't die. They won't listen to a smart person who tells them to stop. They go home and listen to a rapper tell them that they are survivors of the struggle. Have you ever seen a person after they've been shot? There is not one good reason why a person should risk that same situation all over again. It's one thing to say, "Who gives a fuck?" It is definitely something else to have to deal with it. From one minute to the next, you can go from star witness to prime suspect. These days, being a snitch is better than being a victim. Either way, you will always lose in the end. So here's a hint: *when you go out and plot something, make sure you purchase one, too.*

Chapter 4

Crooked System

*W*hat the fuck is this system coming to? Why does it seem to me that society only takes care of the people who don't do shit, leaving the ones who work every day to struggle? A big-time drug dealer or murderer goes to prison to do hard time and comes out with an Associate's degree or a Bachelor of Arts. For free. How the is that possible? I don't want to go to prison, but I still need a degree. Why don't they pay my way through? These same people society considers thugs and drug dealers are being taken better care of than we are as ordinary citizens. Better yet, an inmate gets better treatment upon release than a soldier coming home from war. Is that where my tax money is going? Most of these idiots are only going to take these classes because they want to be out of their cell.

That's also the same reason they go to church. I guess it's the only time church and state really do mix!

The prison system is a bunch of bullshit. Yeah, these inmates do suffer mentally (because they can't be out doing what they are going to continue doing when they get out), but why is a snitch getting less time for a crime others are doing five to ten years for? Fuck snitches. Do you think that, just because he's helping put others in jail, he is actually doing us any favors? There is a big difference between a snitch, a confidential informant, and people who call the cops because they want to clean up their neighborhoods. A snitch and a confidential informant will continue doing the same shit that they are helping put others away for until someone catches up to them. The only positive thing about snitches is that they help cops avoid having to be in a dangerous situation. Fuck that! Lock the snitches up, too. If not, give them a badge and a gun. They're going to need that gun one day.

Sometimes I don't know who is stupider: the follower or the leader. The leader gets the most time for being the mastermind because he got snitched on by his followers, and the followers tell on each other because they're scared. By the time the case is over, twenty people end up in jail for one crime. Guess who gets away with the least time for the crime? The snitch who probably pulled the trigger. Yet people continue to join gangs and trust people who would throw them right in front of a bullet to save themselves. Shit, I'm worth more than a pour of liquor and a tattoo. Don't get me wrong, I used to love the streets. And I'm not telling anyone what to do. But look around; listen to all the ones who are locked up or got out of the game. Everyone has a crazy story about a close call. But if you really think anyone who stands next to you gives a fuck about you, wait and see. One day, you'll either be snitched on or will feel betrayed.

I believe in earning things in life and not giving anything away for free. That's the way everything should be. If you work hard, you should get rewarded for it. If you choose to fuck up, you have to earn your way back into society. If it takes shoveling shit, you should do it with a smile on your face. While an inmate is locked up, he or she will make all kinds of promises and claim some grand transformation, but for most, it's all a show. When they walk out of prison, they act like they never suffered—even though everyone knows they cried every fucking day in prison. That's what I would be doing if I were locked up.

Shit, I love my freedom so much I would probably be on suicide watch every second of my time in a prison. I'm not the one that would go around acting like I wouldn't give a fuck about doing time. And I damn sure wouldn't be claiming that I would do it all over again if I had to. I've worked in a jail and, believe me, I saw some shit I would rather not talk about.

Inmates have always told me that I don't know what it is like to be locked up. They are right; I don't know and never want to know. I don't want to hear shit about prison. I don't care how creative they can be or how many tears they have shed while they were locked up unless they are really trying to change for the better. Other than that, if you commit the crime, no one wants to hear you whine. Suck it up and be as tough as you were when you were free. I don't care how tough anyone acts, being locked up is the closest thing to hell.

Besides, who the fuck wants to be locked up with anyone? Even worse, who wants to get out and then go back to that? I can't even walk into a bathroom at home when someone walks out of it from shittin', never mind having to be locked up for twenty-three hours having to deal with it. I can't even be in a room with a woman for twenty-four hours, why would I want to do it with another man? And imagine doing that for years. And then you have to deal with hearing their bullshit all day about how they are innocent and miss their families. But you know what? Ask them whether they cared about their family when they were out. The only reason they suddenly miss family is because no one else is there for them.

I see all these young kids getting involved in drug and gang activities, but I know that, deep inside, they want to do right. But once they end up in a cell, it is too late to cry for help. And if they think that their boys are going to be the ones paying for their lawyers, writing them letters while they're in jail, coming to visit them to help them get through their worst times ... that's where they're wrong. I'm going to tell you this from experience: everyone I knew who got locked up for years ended up losing their partners and spouses to one of their own boys. No one went to go visit them, no one writes them letters, and no one ever answered their calls. No one cares about you as much as they say they do. You are really stupid if you think that people mean it when they say that they will "ride or die for you". If that's the case, tell them to take the rap for a crime you committed and see how loyal they really are. If your own family can leave you struggling in a cell, what the fuck do you think you're boys are going to do?

You think you can do life in a cell? One name should come to mind: Stanley "Tookie" Williams. This man was big as hell. Not only big, he was also the man who put together one of the most notorious gangs in this country's history. He became even more popular when he was nominated for the Nobel Peace Prize for books he wrote while on death row. What makes you think that you are going to be man enough to throw your entire life away when this man, as crazy and as tough as he was when he was free, decided that the life of crime was not worth it? If you haven't done your history on this man and what he went through while he was locked up, maybe you should. I mean, even the most hardcore criminals who have been doing life in cells regret their acts. What should that tell you? No one in this world would rather be in a cell than be free. Why do people risk losing their freedom and life every day? I have no fucking clue, but they do.

I'm not saying that all inmates are the same, but, most of the ones I have dealt with have ended up going right back to doing the same shit they promised everyone they wouldn't go back to. But yet, the system still believes that these people deserve chance after chance. All I have to say to an inmate is this: If you are going to continue to make all these bullshit promises that you aren't going to follow through with and continue to go in and out of prison, why don't you commit a crime that's going to keep you in there all your life?

That way, you don't have to worry about disappointing the people who actually believe your bullshit.

Chapter 5

Lawyer Up

*B*efore people commit any crimes, they have to know that they're illegal and risky. With that being said, unless a crime is committed in self-defense, that individual chose to place him or herself in a lose-lose situation. And if it is self-defense, you better have all the proof on your side. No one really wins a case in which someone is killed and another one is locked up. There is no situation in which killing another individual is right but, these days, killing another individual is as easy as blinking. Whether you believe me or not, I once faced that situation. There are a few people out there today walking around who I almost chose to kill. All any of those people had to do was cross the street or make one more threat. I'm not a killer, but I do know how easy it is to do it. I've seen it happen, and I have also thought about doing it before. But whether it was me or someone else doing the killing, I don't believe that there should be anyway that one should get one's freedom back for that action. If you kill, you should be locked up forever, unless it was "really" self-defense.

I think that it is hilarious that, when a person is arrested, all they have to say is the word *lawyer* and the questioning has to end. Who the hell came up with that idea? If you actually see a person with a gun or a knife in hand, does he or she really need to be given the opportunity to plead innocent and ask for a lawyer? Does anyone ever think about the victim's family and how they would feel knowing that the suspect could go after them next? If they were so innocent, why would they go on the run? Why would they hide? How come no one knows where they are? Better yet, if they are innocent, why not just turn *themselves* in to prove it? Anytime you have a suspect, chances are high that the person named is the person who committed the crime. Nine out of ten witnesses can't be wrong altogether.

The next stupid thing about the law is bail. Is it about money or is about the safety of the public? Is it really safe to have an accused murderer free days after his or her arrest? Who the fuck is going to monitor that person's daily activities? *All that hard work and the risk that police*

took on to go out and make the arrest results in the sus-
pect walking out with a smile minutes later. What is wrong
with that picture? Only in America, I guess. These lawyers
should feel as guilty as the murderers. Why would anyone
defend a person who is not only guilty, but also lying about
what he or she did? It just doesn't make any sense. When
they ask a suspect to raise his or her right hand and tell the
whole truth, they should also ask the lawyer to do so, too.
After all, a lawyer is constantly looking for holes in a case
to help a criminal go free. Maybe it's because, at the end
of a case, lawyers and judges split the profits.

Why are murderers given the right to post bail but a
terrorist is held without bail and gets tortured for information? A murderer says, "I need my lawyer," and that's
it. Shouldn't a murderer be pressured, too? I would rather
the law be that you freeze the suspect's accounts and keep
the person in prison until they are sentenced or (if they
are lucky) turn out to be innocent. If a person committed
murder or anything close to it, he or she knew that prison
was the only consequence for the act—unless the state car-
ries the death penalty. Why would you allow a person to
go free when, just before he or she got caught, he or she
was considered to be armed and dangerous? Do you think

a few days in a cell is going to make a person change? The first things a person is going to think about doing is getting another gun or going on the run. Do you really think that a person facing life is going to sit around waiting patiently to be sentenced? I guess that's why they call it *bail*. Chances are, that's exactly what they are going to do: flee out of the state.

I strongly favor the three-strike rule. But I believe that, if you end up with three strikes, you should not be allowed any visits while locked up. If they didn't care about the lives of others so many times, why should anyone care about them? Shit, a person is lucky to have three strikes before being sentenced to life in prison. Unfortunately, I will say that I personally know someone who was sentenced on a third strike (repeat offender) who was actually doing much better than he was while growing up. But, like most, a snitch trying to get less time told on him about a past crime they had committed together many years back. I'm not saying that he should be freed by any means, but, his case was an unfortunate one. I knew that he was trying to do better. There are many people I believe really needed one more chance, he is one of them. And, as much as I feel that a person should be put to death for killing someone else, I think that it would be better for him or her to be sentenced to life in prison without the possibility of any type of freedom. I know it sounds fucked up, but they're going to hell anyways—might as well put them through it as quickly as you can.

People who get caught with guns illegally should get a mandatory sentence of ten years. *Especially if they are already considered felons*. Not a one- or five-year sentence. What the fuck is that going to do? Besides that, what the hell do you think they were planning on doing with that gun? It's not for show. A criminal trying to protect himself from another criminal is not self-protection. Had they used it, they would have ended up doing at least twenty-five years anyway. If you do not have a permit to carry or are not law enforcement, you should get locked up. Think of it this way: what if the person didn't get caught with the gun? How many times do you think it has been used before? If gun laws were made to be tougher on people who carry them illegally, we wouldn't have this problem. If bullets cost twenty dollars apiece and had serial numbers inside of them that showed who purchased them, people would probably be a little more responsible.

Chapter 6

Stop Bitching

*H*umans were made strong enough to sustain a lot of physical and emotional pain that will eventually heal. In other words, what doesn't kill you can only make you wiser or stronger. But most importantly, what doesn't kill you shouldn't make you stupid enough to repeat the same mistakes you have already suffered from. The first thing a person must change in life before even starting to try to make a difference in his or her life is the bitching. You can't keep blaming the world or *"the man"* for the shit you create. Many people blame others for issues that they got themselves into. But it's not the issue that's of much concern; *it's how you deal with it that determines the consequences.* It's not up to anyone else but you to do what you should do to make it in life. Second,

39

stop depending on others who don't know you or give a fuck about you to give you a handout.

People are constantly relying on politicians and preachers to help them get where they want to be in life. Why? I don't know. Because if you think that these people really care, you're wrong. They care just as much as actors or musicians who say they love their fans. They don't even know who the fuck you are. Why should they? All they are doing is preaching the Word or going over a written speech that they probably didn't even write and making money. They are not going to change the world by just talking. If you don't get your ass up to do what you have to do in life, you are going to be who and what you have always been: a bum. Answer me this: why is someone who doesn't even know who you are going to help you get what they want for themselves? Let one of them become rich overnight and see whether they will help you tomorrow. But then again, why should they give a fuck about you more than you should care about yourself?

It really sucks that there are positive role models such as Eric Thomas who have been through tough times in life and are really trying to help get others to "wake up" and all people do is criticize them for making it out of the ghetto and being rich. But what most failed to understand was that all they had to do was listen to the words they are preaching. They don't just stand up there as a rich people trying to show off; they stand up there as individuals who want to motivate others toward making better decisions for themselves and their kids. Yet- a bullshit rapper—who no longer lives in the ghetto, who lies all day, who says things that they wouldn't even want their own kids to hear—is considered a better leader to follow. And if that's the case, why are people ending up dead or in jail when trying to live out a rap song?

People give up on politics and religion because most live in the present. They want results yesterday. All those promises that politicians make are no different than an inmate making promises to their loved ones from a cell. Nothing is ever going to change. Politicians have been making all kinds of promises to people since the beginning of time. But what have they really done? Gotten rich! That's it. Just like a preacher. It sucks that I have to say that, but it is true. No one even cares about politics these days. I can't say the same about religion because people have a better shot at getting what they want from a prayer than they do from a politician who doesn't give a fuck if a soldier makes it back home dead or alive. All a politician really does is play the public like puppets. The leaders of this country aren't even focused on this country anyway. Similar to when Trump said, grab them by the pussy, they all got us by the balls.

All I have ever wanted was to have enough money to travel and see the entire world. I have always wanted to go anywhere I wanted from one day to the next and enjoy life to the fullest. That's not my reality, but you don't see me bitching about anything. Shit, I lived the life of a *Loser* early in life, and now I'm paying the price for it. But everywhere I go, all I hear are these fucking punks talking about how hard life is and how they wish they could be rich and not have to work. Shut the fuck up, get a job, and grow up. And then you'll see that life is not all about having money. Worry about having a roof over your head first and then plan whatever it is you want to do in life. Because I'll be honest: I'm not the luckiest person in the world—and to my knowledge, none of my prayers have been answered—but I try to use my past as motivation and move forward each day. I can't rewind time or buy my time back that I wasted. But bitching isn't going to help. One thing I'm not going to do is go back to selling drugs to make a little more money. I'm not trying to end up in a cell with a fucking punk who's going to be crying all night for a Bible he won't even understand.

Isn't it a little crazy that people have to go through hell to find God? After all, as long as they are getting by doing whatever it is they like to do, nothing matters to them more than what makes them happy. Once they get into some shit, they go reaching for a Bible or a pen to write a statement helping the same cops they hated prior to getting locked up. All of a sudden, cops become their best friends. But you already know why that is: everyone has a little bitch in them. As soon as they see that they are about to lose their freedom or life, they will give up their best friends just like that. Inmates always say that they have changed and they will never go back to prison. Put guns, some alcohol, or their choice of drugs in front of them, however, and then tell me what you think about them.

These people who say they'll never go back to prison or using or selling drugs are only temporarily rehabilitated. As soon as they get out of jail, the first thing they do is hang out with the same people as before. Once they take that first hit or make that first illegal dollar, they're on their way back to prison. Once they end up in a cell, it's the world's fault. All you hear is bitching about how they are inno-cent and that they don't deserve years in prison all over again. Answer this: what other punishment can replace doing prison time? How about a coffin? That's the next step. That way, no one has to deal with you bitching all day.

The only time people actually listen is when they get something in return for it. Everyone lives for today. I mean, look at how uninterested people really are until they get something in return. Many people these days live check to check, but using up that last check may be one step from being homeless. But try living hand-to-mouth next to a dumpster with a can full of change, and I guarantee you that you'll stop bitching about your life compared to others who have far less. The bottom line is this: learn from your mistakes and don't repeat them—but if you do, handle it like the man you think you are. No one in this world owes you anything.

Until then, keep bitching and snitching.

All you're doing is creating jobs and keeping people employed.

Chapter 7

Grow Up

First off, let me tell you that I am probably what one would call a true asshole. I have no problem denying that. I can be a little extreme once in a while, but the reason for me being this way is easy to explain. Because I live a simple life, I want my days to go very smoothly. And if others decide that they want to waste my time by bringing bullshit into my life, I make it clear to them that their presence will no longer be needed. If there's a lot of history between us, there's a chance that I will forgive and forget eventually. But once anyone crosses me, it is going to be very difficult for us to get back to where we were. That's why I don't deal with many people. I try my hardest to avoid as many people as I can because I will be the first person to say that I am not the easiest to get along with. Better yet, I don't want to hear about people's prob-lems or ever want to end up dealing with them somehow.

Here is the only reason why I try my hardest not to do anything wrong: aside from my fear of being locked up or getting shot, I honestly believe that people may end up in hell if they choose to live a criminal life. I'm not saying that I would love to kill someone, but violence crosses most of our minds in reaction to other people's ignorance. As much as I have wanted to fuck up some-body for crossing me, all I do now is walk away pissed off, trying to ignore the situation the best way I can. No one would fuck with me if they were able to read my mind and see the things that I thought about doing to them afterward. I'm not trying to act like I'm the toughest man alive—I'm not. I'm speaking from the point of view of having to deal with people who have nothing else to do than make other people's lives as miserable as theirs.

There is nothing in this world that pisses me off more than ignorance. There is nothing worse than an adult who acts like a kid. No matter how much you try to let him or her know that he or she is acting immature or ignorant, the more that person seems to resist the idea. People get pissed off at you for telling them the truth. If you see me out in public and I look like I'm trying to ignore you, chances are that's exactly what I am doing. I'm very aware of my surroundings. I probably saw you and turned my attention somewhere else so I wouldn't have to hear about all the problems you are dealing with. I can't even ask a person how they are doing these days because it will be like confession on a Sunday. If you need someone to talk to, you can usually look in the mirror and get better answers than you would get from me or anyone else dealing with worse issues than you are. This is especially true if you are an inmate or criminal who needs to give up the life of crime or stay in prison the rest of your life.

What could be worse than having to deal with individuals who act like they don't care whether they are free in society or locked up in prison? It makes no difference to them because they are treated better in prison than they are in society. And you know whose fault that is?

The people who created the current system. You know how, in a store, the customer is always right? These days, inmates are getting the same treatment because wardens don't want to deal with inmates acting out of control. Because they don't want to deal with the headache, they treat them with care. And you know who has to suffer in the end: society. These people who couldn't care less about being in prison are getting the best of both worlds. And then they go right back to the streets and fuck up what others have tried their hardest to keep straight. Meanwhile, I have to shut up or get shot when trying to pull out my license and registration.

A bullet does not care about how real or how fake you are. Those who claim to be real usually get so comfortable living off their reputations that they don't realize that the same terrible things can and will happen to them. And the fake ones end up in a cell crying like bitches because they never really had it in them to do life in a cell. They just felt that life was all about entertainment and had to prove to others that they were capable of doing what their boys were doing. First of all, real or fake, you'll end up dead or locked up. If you're lucky, you'll end up in a wheelchair. I don't know what's so lucky about that, but at least you're still alive. No matter what, however, you lose. Chances are you'll end up at a funeral home, getting a ride to the cemetery, and waiting for your soul to fly you to your next destination.

Growing up, I used to think that, once you reached a certain age, you were automatically considered an adult.

Just for the hell of it, let me explain what an *adult* is to me. Being an adult means that you are responsible and in total control of the choices and decisions you make in your life. It also means that, if you are able to get your ass off the bed and able to work, you should. But if you are just sitting on a project bench, standing on a corner, sitting around gossiping about other people's business, or bitching all day and expecting a handout, you're just a fucking loser. You're a first-class loser who depends on freebies or some kind of aid just to get by. A few years later, you'll be standing in front of a store being ignored by customers while begging for change. I'm sure that those who are struggling today never thought they would be. But people choose where they end up in life. Unless there's an accident or something caused naturally, everything in life is a choice.

Nothing gets to me more than people who waste their time trying to find the easiest ways to make it through their lives while making other people's lives harder. If you have lived a shitty life by choice, suck it up and deal with it. Stop acting like your issues are other people's obligations. I'm pissed that my life isn't as perfect as I would love it to be, but do you know what I choose to do? I choose to stay out of everyone else's business. I don't sit around and point the finger at others like I'm better than anyone else. Everyone, regardless of how they may seem, has issues. People may have good days, but they don't have perfect lives. No one does. You can't just keep on blaming cops, judges, and politicians all your life.

I don't model my life around anyone. I do the best that I can with the life I could have made better. I do what I do because it makes my days and my life simple. There is nothing to it. All I want out of life is for people to leave me alone unless they really need something important from me. Here is all I need: a twelve-pack of Heineken, a Yankees game, ESPN, my two sons, and my fiancé to finally understand me. I don't want to have to deal with answering those stupid *who, what, where, when,* or *why* questions for anyone anymore. I want everyone around me to live their lives however they choose to. I don't want to have any say in how others live their lives, and I expect the same in return. I just want to be married one day with the understanding that men and women think differently.

But in the end, I want my boys to see their parents together forever.

Like I have.

Chapter 8

Carried by Six

*L*ife in the streets comes at you faster than you can ever imagine. There's no time to think and barely any time to react. From one minute to the next, your life can go from bad to worse without warning. Most of us fail due to reacting without thinking. A person who lives the street life will at one time or another run into a situation in which their life or freedom is threatened. From one second to the next, one's reactions determine where one will end up. Although many will tell you that they will do whatever they have to do to survive, in reality, it's all about who gets to whom first. Either way, both sides lose.

No person in this world knows their own body until he or she must face a situation that is not up to him or her. People figure out that they may not be as mentally or physically tough as they always thought they were. Why do you think people break down when facing something they have never experienced before? People will cry, throw up, pass out, go on the run, and even attempt suicide when facing a matter their minds and bodies have never experienced. For example, how can anyone mentally or physically prepare to live life in a wheelchair or in a prison? There is no practice for these things. Many say that they will do whatever they have to, but once they are in the situation, their thinking changes.

Having been on the streets for almost twenty years of my life, I know how hard it is to be smart and do the right thing. If you allow someone to threaten you or disrespect you (and you don't do what's expected of you), the same people that you consider friends can't trust you to be there for them if they face the same situation. So what do these people do? They react violently by doing things they know they don't want to do. I had a guy tell me one day that he would rather be judged by twelve than to be carried by six. He is now doing life. I know that neither option is great, but I also know that you can't control how or when you are going to die or be killed. Nine times out of ten, you can or should be able to control a situation before you actually make the decision to kill. Personally, I would rather be carried by six than to be judged by twelve. That's not me being tough, that's just me saying that I never want to be locked up in a cell to learn a lesson for the rest of my life that I could have prevented or controlled.

Don't get me wrong, there are some crazy violent people out there who truly do not give a fuck. If you do not believe me, watch a few episodes of *Gangland*. There are some people who live their lives in the fast lane, and the only two things that will stop them are bullets or prison. These kinds of people, unless they get tired of doing what they do and change, will keep going until something they can't control stops them. Most of the time, even they know that what they are doing is wrong; they're just not patient enough to make it the harder way.

You will never see a person's truest feelings that are held really deep inside until they are locked up for life. And by *life*, I mean no chance of parole. When people are stripped of all things they became accustomed to, waking up without them will eventually take its toll on them. I've faced many situations in which it wasn't until after the incident that I began to think of the people I would have missed had I ended up locked up. It's those split second decisions that will have you regretting a lifetime of suffering. I know this does not compare to prison time, but I have been bored many times at home. And that's being free. I can't imagine being in a cell. Call me a punk, call me a bitch—in fact, call me scared. When it comes down to it, I would rather be all three while free than to be all three while locked up. Like I have always said, people are never themselves until they are by themselves. With a gun or with a crew, anyone can be tough, but alone in a cell where no one can see you crying, you become a completely different person.

If you can honestly say that you don't give a fuck about losing your life or freedom, chances are the situation will eventually occur whereby you will have to prove it. But it shouldn't have to be like that. You should want to be free. You should want to live. What is life worth if you can't control your own choices and decisions? Sign number one that a person does care about life and freedom is when a suspect pleads innocent in a courtroom. If they really didn't care, they wouldn't waste people's time with lies and excuses. It's not until you sit back in a cell and begin to think of other ways you could have handled the situations you faced that you will realize how much freedom is really worth. It's been years since I have hung out on the streets. Things have changed for the worse. But one situation really makes me wonder what I would do. When someone gets shot, they claim they don't know who did it. Most don't want to be known as a snitch, and would rather go after the person and end up in prison permanently. What would you do? I would probably pull a *Fresh Prince* move and leave town to change for the better.

I've never been able to make any sense of why inmates would fight so hard to be free only to put themselves right back into situations where they end up losing their freedoms or even their lives. I can go back to saying that certain people may be afraid of being referred to as punks for doing the right things in life, but why should proving themselves to others by losing their freedom or life be more important than changing for the better? No matter how you look at it, that makes no sense. When you're locked up, none of the people you thought would be there for you will even attempt to visit. How many times do you actually think they'll show up to visit you at a cemetery? *Maybe when they end up right next to you.*

From what I have been through in my life, I have figured out that mostly everyone only for cares about themselves. I'm not saying that others *should* be more important, but regardless of how much people tell you to trust them or that they will be there for you in a time of need, you can't be sure. It's not until you are at the bottom and have nothing or nowhere to go that you will see who truly cares for you. Most of the times the people who actually show up to help are people you may have never expected to be there for you. Not your boys. You won't realize these things until they actually happen. If nothing that you are reading helps, understand this: your boys will only be your boys if you are down with losing your freedom and life. Your real friends will encourage and even help you to do the right things in life. It may take longer to get what you would like to achieve doing it the right way. But why risk your freedom or life over materialistic things or over being disrespected?

Certain things work for certain people; you should do what works for you. No one in this world should tell you what's best for you unless it is something positive. One thing that helped me change was asking me how I would describe myself to someone else. When I realized that most of the things I would have said were all negative, I knew that I had a lot of changes to make in my life. Not that I was living a fucked up life, but I wasn't happy with myself. I wasn't making wise decisions. I had been my own enemy for most of my life. If you don't have an idea of what you will be doing in the next five years, you are only setting yourself up for failure for at least the next ten.

Being locked up in a prison is no different than laying in a cemetery: you are dead to the world.

Chapter 9

Mama's Drama

I have been trying to figure out for years why it is that a lot of women these days think that the loser men they choose at a bar or on a corner are going to be the ones to take them away from their struggles and out of their misery. These guys love the streets. They love the street life because of the easy money and easy women. They are going to continue to do the same thing most men do these days: become a deadbeat dad. Unless you have been living in a cave for the past ten or fifteen years, you should know that, these days, there are many kids running around without a father. Shit, all you have to do is watch a documentary. But you really don't even have to do that. There is probably a live episode going on right next door to you. If you don't understand what I mean, it is really simple to explain: there are no taxes being taken out of drug money profit, and you won't be able to get child support from someone who is not working or locked up.

It's really sad that, before some of these kids are even born, the mother is confused about who the father is. Is it even embarrassing anymore not to keep track of the people you've slept with? This shit happens so much these days it's almost considered normal—like fucking someone else just to get the ex-mad is okay. I don't know who should be embarrassed more, though: the father or the mother. When the mother finds out the one she thought was the father isn't the one, she immediately claims she now knows who it really is. But when the father hears that he's the daddy, he jumps up and hugs the mother. But wait a minute; wasn't she confused just a second ago? Doesn't that mean that she was fucking somebody else? Or are they both just that stupid? I understand that the truth offends a lot of people. I also understand why a lot of people choose to keep their mouths shut rather than to say anything because they feel they may offend others. But there are people who really need to hear the truth sometimes.

It's kind of hard to choose where to assign the blame. People always seem to blame it on the easy women. But at the same time, I don't know what the hell these guys are thinking either. Are they just fucking without a condom and falling asleep? If you can have sex with someone on the first night or on any night for that matter without a condom, what makes you think you were the first one to do so? I don't care how good a person looks when you're sober or drunk, try using a fucking condom. Does anyone actually think of all the risks they are running anymore? Not everyone has a Magic Johnson, if you know what I mean. Although some may have been a little lucky and never ended up with some type of life-ending disease, they still left kids in the world who will never have a father. Luckily, chlamydia is curable because, if it weren't, there would be a lot of people in trouble right now. Some people I knew thought that it was a big joke to just swallow the chalky drink at Planned Parenthood and get back to fucking raw.

These days, one mother brings in five or six different grandmothers into one family. How crazy is that? Do they even know that the entire town talks about women who have many kids with different men? They call these women chicken heads, hoes, and tricks, just to name a few. What's crazy is that most of these women have the nerve to just sit around all day talking about everyone else's business. It's as if there existed such a thing as a classy ho. Liquor and drugs do make people do things that they normally wouldn't do when they were sober, but a child you will later claim as a regret or a mistake is as irresponsible as you can get. There really is no excuse. I don't care how much you had to drink, smoke, or sniff. Making kids should be planned; it should be a gift to you. Some of these women need to think back and remember when their pussies were their most sacred body parts. These days, it's easier to get a piece of ass than it was to get a simple kiss when we were young.

It's sad to say, but sixteen or eighteen years from the day the kid is born, the parents may be in a courtroom watching them get sentence or on a stretcher trying to fight for life. As men, we have to seriously own up to our choices. It's really sad to see a child having to go through struggles simply because the parents never planned properly. They are human lives. I think about my sons every single day and I am proud to say that I love them with no regrets. I just don't know how anybody can sleep at night knowing that they have a kid out there that they aren't taking care of. Unfortunately, they will end up being misled by others who may have also been abandoned at a young age.

Before you make the choice you will later claim to be a mistake, think about the fact that you will not be able to afford taking care of that child. Think of the years that child will struggle while not knowing who his or her father was. Think of the embarrassing moments that child will go through when every other kid shows up with both parents to school functions. At the same time, if you're out there selling drugs or committing crimes, understand that you may be locked up or dead and will never be able to be there for your children.

You know, they say it's cheaper to keep them when they are referring to child support.

But you know what's even cheaper than not paying child support?

A three-dollar pack of condoms.

Chapter 10

Rather Be Single

*I*sn't it weird how, when you're in a relationship, you sometimes wish you were single? And then, when you're single, you feel like you're living a boring and depressing life. Or maybe that's just how I feel. I've had the worse luck with finding love and staying in a relationship. Sometimes I think I've found it only to find out we weren't the perfect match. Of course, everyone would love to find that one person with whom they can be happy. But in order to maintain a relationship, you have to make it a priority over other things you feel are as important. It's like practice for marriage: do this, do that, I need this, I need that. Fuck that. I hate to say this, but if you don't allow a person some time to do what they like to do or to be themselves, your relationship has a great chance of failing.

I loved being single. But when I'm in a relationship, I like to do the same things I did when I was single. In other words, I still do whatever makes me happy. If I want to go out, I just go; if I need some alone time, that's what I expect to get. Maybe that's the reason why my relationships never lasted as long as they should have. But before you pass judgment on me, understand that the same applies for the person I'm with. I am not the controlling type; I want my partner to go and enjoy her life however she wants. But because of all the trust issues people have these days; it has become more and more difficult for anyone to step out the door without being accused of cheating. There are two things about trust you need to understand: what you don't know won't hurt you, but if you know a person has cheated on you and you don't leave them, there is a great chance that you will continue to get hurt.

One thing that people fail to understand is that, prior to getting in a relationship, they had lives. And you should never stop living how you like just because you're in a relationship. Put it this way: you had a life before you got into a relationship, and you're going to have it if you break up. No one in this world should ever feel like they are somebody's parent. If you allow people to control you, sooner or later, they'll be smacking you around like you're a kid instead of a partner. Once you give someone the power to tell you what to do or where to go, you will never be happy. I've heard people say stupid shit—"I got roughed up, but it was all out of love"—but they need to wake up to what's really happening. If you are in a relationship in which you have to ask permission to do things, you're setting yourself up for failure. Not only is the relationship not going to work, it will also limit you to accomplishing most of your plans and goals in your life. If you have to start a fight just to go out, do yourself a favor and just stay out. You'll end up looking back at your past and noticing how much you could have done if you would have just done what was right for you.

Every relationship should be different. You can't go into a relationship expecting that you don't have to meet each other halfway. Love is blind, but if you can't see eye to eye, it will never work. The best partners to have are the ones who will tell you that they really don't need you for shit. Or the ones who will tell you that if things don't work out they can make it without you. Most claim to be independent but can never stop asking for a favor. But the ones that are so used to doing things on their own are the responsible ones who will dedicate themselves to making things right for themselves and their partners. Nevertheless, there has to come a time when you give in and do whatever it takes to make your partner as happy as they try to make you. The problem is that most people interpret people's kindness for weakness, especially when they feel they have the upper hand.

If you spend too much time together, someone is going to want space. If you don't spend enough time together, someone is going to accuse each other of cheating or crying about not being loved. One side is never going to be fully satisfied. And then you start hearing shit like, "You don't love me like I love you," or, "Why aren't things like they used to be in the beginning?" I'll tell you why. The best parts of relationships occur in the first few months, the honeymoon stage. After that, you just hope that you can deal with or adapt to each other's ways. The reason why people seem so into each other at first is because they keep all their bullshit to themselves until they feel comfortable telling you about their problems. Relationships are just like job interviews. You're always going to say what a person wants to hear, but, once you get to know each other, that's when the real you comes out. The hardest part of it all is to come to terms that you were both raised differently and have gone through different things. Coming together as one might not be as easy as you would expect.

This is my way of getting around the bullshit with relationships. First of all, I don't have game. I'm not the kind of person to go around lying or buying drinks just to get phone numbers or a piece of ass. I'm a little old school: I would rather hear about someone who likes me or wants to be with me, and then I can decide whether l want anything to do with that person. That way, going in, you know that the other person likes you. You don't have to sit around and lie to each other just to get together. The worst relationships to be in are the ones with people who got so used to having it their way with others in the past and then expect you to just accept that reality. And then there's the rebound shit. Fuck that, too. I can't deal with people who think they have to be spoiled in order to stay happy. That's a vibe killer from the start.

Want to know when it is not love? If you can't deal with a person not answering your calls, if they have you riding around town looking for him or her, if you're lying in your bed wondering where the person is, or if you can't sleep until you hear from him or her, that's when you're in trouble. It's called being infatuated. No matter how tough you act or how much control you think you have, once you have to go chasing after your partner and try to make things right, the bitch in you will come out eventually. And then you have to work on trying to change your ways. When they are finally fed up, there's nothing else you can do but lay right back on the bed crying, reminiscing, and regretting. Love shouldn't make you have to go through all that. Real love is different. But when you fuck up real love, trust me when I tell you that you will never really know what you had until someone else is fucking your ex.

Real love is very hard to find these days. It's not what it used to be. I remember back in the days when a crush actually meant something. Nowadays, people seem to just want to fuck. If you think people used to try their hardest to not get caught cheating, social media has made it a lot easier for them to be even sneakier. They'll do it right there in front of you and you probably won't even realize it. You want to know if they are cheating or being sneaky, simply see their crazy ass reaction when you ask to see their phone. That alone will tell you everything you need to know. I don't think that things will ever get back to how they used to be when it comes to relationships because people aren't as patient as they used to be. One argument or disagreement and they are in boxing the next person that they already had in line to replace you. If not, they are on their phones all day not even paying you any attention. I believe that friendship and conversations are the only things that will keep couples happy in a relationship. In fact, it is the key to happiness. Without that, your relationship will barely stand a chance.

Chapter 11

I'm Not Perfect

They say no one is perfect. But you can damn sure try to be. I try to have the most perfect days every day I wake up. My way of trying to accomplish that is by doing as little as possible. I am a simple person. But somewhere in the middle, there always seems to be something that appears out of nowhere to fuck things up. I try to ignore a lot and, at the same time, react in a way that it won't show any of my negative emotions. But all that seems to do is pile up and make me even more prone to blow up. I don't know what it is but, for some reason or another, disruptions continue to appear out of the blue. I believe that some people just can't live without drama. They love arguing and fighting. Without it in their lives, it seems as though they are bored and can't make it through a day without it. Then, when you've had enough and react, they turn everything on you and make it seem like you're the one who instigated it all.

I don't ever remember needing anyone like people have needed me. It's like I'm everyone's shoulder to lean on when they have problems. Sometimes I feel like I'm being punished for all the shit I put others through in the past. But damn, how long do I have to keep dealing with this? I must be the only person in the world who doesn't want any more friends. Friends these days create most of the issues that we have to deal with. I know for sure I went wrong somewhere in my past—I had every opportunity to get out of my neighborhood when I was younger. I could have been in the majors playing baseball had I listened to my father. As crazy as it may sound, I could have been out enjoying my life in any country had I joined the military when they came knocking on my door. I probably would be running from a few bullets in a war somewhere, but the same shit was happening to me on the street corners of my neighborhood.

It took many years, but I had to change my negative ways. I did what everyone should do when they find themselves in a hole. See, when we live a negative life, we tend to get rid of the positive people we should keep near. But those who live a positive life just keep pushing away the negative ones. This was not the easiest thing for me to do, but I had to do it. There was no way in the world I was going to be able to reach any goal, stay out of prison, or avoid getting shot had I not changed my ways. Ultimately, I just shut down and tried my hardest to stay away from people, places, and things that were going to prevent me from changing my life. When you find yourself in some shit you can't get out of, it's always the ones you thought you never needed who are going help you—not the ones who just want you to be losers like them. See how they react when they see you doing better than them, and you'll understand fully what I'm trying to say. Go find a job and work for the "white man", for example (who else are you going to work for when most of us minorities don't really own shit or trust our own?) And then see how people treat you.

Most people don't believe my stories about the past. I don't have a record to show that I was actually doing illegal and negative things. But is that a good or a bad thing? I thought the object of the game was to get away with shit. Fuck a street reputation. That shit is not going to get me to the next level in my life. I would rather work for "the man" than be chased by him. Those out on the streets have an odd way of thinking: if it's not the white man trying to lock them up, it's the white man not giving them a job. Who the fuck put drugs and guns into your hands? Who the fuck wanted to take the easy way out? That excuse about growing up in a negative environment is understandable, but people don't want to hear that shit these days. Would you hire a con if you owned your own business? All you're doing is wasting time by complaining. If you didn't have a track record longer than your employment history, it wouldn't be that hard to find a job.

Personally, I don't bother anyone for anything. I could be broke and would rather starve than ask someone for a favor. I've been there many times in my life. But it's my entire fault: I spend way too much money on bullshit and, by the end of the week, I'm fucked. It's what makes me happy, though. In my life, I have always thought I was going to live a short life anyway. I have to snap out of that, though, because I'm way past what I thought would have been my due date. I remember one day staring at a pork chop in a garbage can at my brother's house. I had no money and I hadn't had anything to eat the entire day. You have no idea how close I was to digging it out of there and eating it. In reality, that was all I needed to go through to realize that if I didn't change my ways, digging in cans would become my way of survival. You live, you listen, and (hopefully) you learn. Fortunately for me, I've lived through and experienced many of the things others just see or hear about. What saves me is that I can apply anywhere without having to tell them that I'm a convicted felon.

Tunnel vision is more or less how I try to remain focused on my path and future. I try to avoid anything and anyone that will distract me from moving forward. But I must admit that it is very difficult to break away from old habits, especially as an adult. It is very difficult for me because it seems like, while I'm changing my ways, others take my kindness for weakness. And then I become more frustrated because I'm making a change in my life for others to feel comfortable around me. In return, all I get is the bullshit. I just end up regretting that I tried to change not only for others, but also to avoid feeling stressed out every day. It's like a no-win situation for me. If I help out, it's like feeding stray cats: they just keep coming back. If I don't, I'm an asshole. I wish I could just say fuck the world and everything in it, but that's not going to help. It sounds like I bitch a lot, but believe me, I know there are a lot of people who feel the same way. I know there are people who have to deal with the same types of people and the same type of shit as I do.

Some people wake up with plans for quick results. Others wake up trying to accomplish goals they've set for their future. Many others pray all day for change. I'm just happy to make it through every day and night without getting into some type of problem with someone. You can say that I am somewhat uptight, but I'm always aware of what goes on around me. My mentality has always been to be prepared for anything at all times. After all, it seems like things happen to people when they get comfortable and least expect it. When I was younger, we used to walk around looking for people to start problems with. Of course, I regret all of the stupid and ignorant things I used to do, but if it is true when they say that what goes around comes back around, at least I can say I'm always ready for it.

I have always pictured someone coming out of nowhere and trying to kill me. I've done a lot of fucked up things in my life to other people. But because of that fear, I am always looking out for anything out of the norm. If I see it coming before it actually happens, I may be able to get away from the situation in time. But if I don't and have to react without thinking, there's nothing to do about that. I have to protect myself. Regardless of the consequences, I come first. No cop or judge would sit back and allow anyone to put them in a life-or-death situation and stifle the wish that they had done something to save themselves. Unfortunately, the system wouldn't even give a fuck if I were trying to protect myself. But like I have always said, some people deserve certain things. I'm no exception.

Although I put myself through this, I need to sit back and reflect on my past and think of ways to change my ways toward people. That would allow me to understand that I shouldn't take people or time for granted. Lately, I have tried my hardest to understand that what bothers me most about people may be an overreaction. I'm still young and have a lot of personal adjustments to make. I'm trying not to be the antisocial person I have been for a very long time now. I have to stop thinking that everyone is out to get me. There are people out there who may actually care about me.

I just don't want to have to deal with issues any-more. I have been dealing with problems most of my life. Sometimes I wish I could be a people person; I wish I didn't have to be an asshole. I actually consider myself a good and honest person, though. One thing people can't say about me is that I don't have a heart. I give when people are in need and help out when someone needs a hand. But when I know people can do things on their own and don't, that bothers me the most.

I know I could have done better in my past. Shit, I could be doing a lot better today. But I want to do what makes me happy; I want to enjoy my life by doing the simple things. I'm tired of people using me. I'm tired of people bitching to me about things they could have avoided. I guess that, as long as I am out of a prison cell, I should be happy. I'm not perfect and will never be. You really can't blame me for what I have become throughout the years. These days, you can't just let people take advantage of you; you have to be able to control your own destiny. If you let one person misguide you, you will end up regretting everything in your past like I have. My main point is that you should always mind your own business and never get involved in other people's issues. Like they say, if one person is drowning, don't just jump in and make it two.

Chapter 12

Soul Searching

*A*t this time, I am still young and trying to enjoy life the best that I can. But not one day passes by that I don't wonder how much longer I have left. Not that I'm in a hurry to go, but I do think about it a lot. Sometimes I feel like I don't do enough just in case that time does come sooner than expected. Although I talk a lot about death, I am actually a little scared to die. Not because I fear what's going to happen to me when I die, but because I am going to miss the ones I love and care about. I wonder who will miss me and who will show up at my wake and funeral. Who's going to be that one bold person to stand up and say something they remembered about me? I wonder where I will end up, too. One of the things that I would love to know is how my life is going to end. Is it going to be a natural death, or is it going to be tragic? Is it going to be painful, or is it going to happen peacefully?

This may be a little strange for many, but no matter how long it takes, I cannot wait to see what really happens when we die. I wonder what things will be like and where we'll end up. We live in a very beautiful world now; I can't even imagine what the after-life would be like. (I hope that there is such thing as heaven.) I hope that we don't just live life, die, and that's it. I guess it's one of those things we just have to sit back and await. It's not that I don't believe in a God, it's just that I don't believe anyone has proof either way. I think that most people think about these things at one point or another. Is there really a heaven? What about hell? Does the devil really exist? How can people claim to know this? I've read parts of the Bible and Qur'an, and a lot of it sounds a little unbelievable. And it's not so much that I am trying to disrespect the stories I have read, I just think that there are people who try so hard to turn others into believers that they exaggerate a little. Sometimes I think people get caught up trying to interpret certain things that only leave most of us confused about religion and its truths.

All I know is this: we live and we die. It's the saddest thing we will ever have to deal with or go through. But is it the worst that could happen to us? Yes, we do suffer from having to deal with losing people we love, but are they in a better place? The only thing we can say is that we hope so. There is no need to go through this type of punishment and then end up with nothing. Most of the people I know who are no longer with us either died too young or died tragically. Do these things happen for a reason? I thought life was supposed to be a gift given to us. Why could it be taken away so tragically from us in an instant? It always seems like it's the ones we care about most who are being taken from us. Why is it that the ones who constantly put themselves in danger (and probably deserve death) are still living?

You'll never know how much a person really means to you until he or she is no longer there. Believe me when I tell you that it is the worse type of pain a person ever has to live through. Sometimes you'll be sitting around and a thought comes to mind as if the past were brought to life, and then you snap out of it and end up choking in tears. I've found myself speechless at the cemetery. Those deep thoughts will have you wishing you could rewind time and have done things differently. I celebrate their birthdays or the anniversaries of their deaths at the cemetery. All I hope for is that they can hear me while I'm there. It's very hard to be normal or to think straight when you lose someone you loved and cared about. Sometimes it even has you wishing that you could trade places with that person—especially when the last days weren't how you wish they were. It is the most regretful feeling you'll ever deal with. Although it may not be the best approach, you can just sit back, shut down for a while, and work your way back slowly. Sometimes it has taken me about a week to start thinking straight again after I go through my rough times of reminiscing.

There are so many people I miss. I wish I would have done a lot more with them while they were here. It's not easy losing someone you never expected to go so soon. But like I said, for all we know, they are in a better place. It can't get any worse than this hell we live in. I'm not saying that life itself is worthless, but the shit we have to deal with just to make it is fucked up. And things continue to get worse. I'm sure God didn't put us here for this. I've been hearing that Jesus was coming soon since I was about five years old. Given how crazy this world is today, I wouldn't doubt it if He made it halfway and just turned right back around. He would probably rather wait for us one by one than to deal with the craziness we are all dealing with together. Sometimes I sit around and wonder what the last days would be like. What would happen afterward? In some ways, I want to see whether things are going to occur how these preachers have been saying they will. You hear preachers talking about it like they know for sure. I suppose my biggest hope is that I end up in a better place than where I am now.

Chapter 13

Black Cat

My luck has never been all that great. Even when I have had the opportunity to experience something I never thought I would, I have found more ways than one to fuck it up for myself. I've had many opportunities to get away and pursue every goal I've had since I was kid. For some, life gets worse every day; for others, it gets better or stays the same. As for me, I try to remain focused on surviving every day. I don't plan anything in my life. I guess you can say that's the reason why my life has not changed in the past few years, but at least I am alive. My reason for never planning anything is because I would rather just go with the flow of life instead of having to face failure ever again. I tend to focus more on the bigger picture. And to me, that entails just living and trying to enjoy every day and everything as much as I can while I'm here.

Many people I know who keep trying every day fail because they only focus on one thing. And that's how I used to be. But every time I've tried, I either lost or failed. My dreams have turned to fantasies that became illusions. The older I got, the further my dreams drifted. Every day for me is like going up a step ladder that just keeps getting higher and higher. But I'm willing to climb as high as I can and hope I don't fall. I don't focus on money or the wishes that everyone has of having a big house and a nice car. Those things come with patience and hard work. Of course, you can try to get them the easy way but, chances are, you will only enjoy those quick results temporarily. Many of us tried it and many of us failed. In fact, I can honestly say that I have more these days through hard work than I had when we were trying to make easy money. Once I learned that I didn't have to have thousands of dollars in my pocket or to depend on a drug addict to come around so I can pay my bills, I understood that the value of life supersedes the value of a dollar. What good is a dollar if you can't enjoy it? Jail just wasn't for me.

Sometimes I feel like I have had the worse luck in the world. I always seem to end up in situations that I told myself I would never get back into ever again. But for some reason, I guess I can't change some of the things that have kept me from moving forward. I've had the worst luck with friends, with money, with consequences, and relationships. No matter how well I plan things, they never seem to come out how I would hope. That's why I have decided to just say, "Fuck it." I will live and deal with whatever comes in the best way that I can. If things don't come out right, I'll try something else tomorrow. What's crazy is that I've had better things happen when I've stopped trying to pursue the things that were probably not meant for me to have. A lot of the time, that's exactly the case. Many say that God has a plan for all of us, and if something is not part of the plan for you, you will fail. Like they say, if it weren't for bad luck I wouldn't have any luck at all.

One of the biggest lessons that I have learned is that, when you leave something behind that never comes out right and you end up going back to it over and over again, something will always remind you of why you left it in the first place. Some things are just not meant to be. Think about it: if they say that things happen for a reason, why not believe that when things don't work out that maybe you should just try something else? It doesn't matter what it is—if your relationship isn't working out and you keep trying to force it to work, it's never going to work. If you're a drug dealer who has been in and out of prison, you need to find a new way to make your money, especially if you've been shot trying to make it. If life were based on failure, we would all lose. That's why you have a lifetime to try new things. Sometimes you have to stop and ask yourself *"Am I doing the best that I can with myself?* "If you are satisfied with what you are doing, no one in this world should stop you from being happy. The only thing that should keep you from trying harder is physical limitations.

I've gone so far down the wrong path in my life that I thought it would be a complete waste of time to go back and start all over again. So I just stopped right where I was at and decided that enough was enough. I changed everything. The one thing I failed to do was plan what I was going to do to make up for all of my lost time. I had no plans, no ideas, and no help. I felt like a smoker or an alcoholic who wanted to stop cold turkey. But after a while, I realized that I couldn't make up for wasted time. The only time I ever try to look back is when I come across a similar situation I have faced in my past—and then I try to deal with it differently. No matter what has happened in my life, I never gave up. I didn't give up because I knew that tomorrow's issues could be a lot tougher than yesterday's. If you look at your issues as a challenge, it will make the next obstacle easier to deal with.

I don't know if you have any idea what it is like to try to change your ways without a plan but, believe me when I tell you, it is definitely a challenge. What's worse about it is that the people you decide to separate yourself from seem to become your enemies overnight. It's like they get offended because you are trying to lead your life in a new direction. I don't want to place blame on anyone, but they're half the reason why I had to change. I followed the wrong people in my life, so I had to change friends to make things right. Friends shouldn't let friends fuck up. Those kinds of friends just want to be failures together. Because once you try to do the right thing, they will turn their backs on you instantly.

I'm a very stubborn person. I don't like to show emotions when I'm down—never mind when I'm hurt. My biggest problem is that I always try to act like everything is all right regardless of the situation. That's the only thing I have had the most issues with changing. In life, you have to learn to sacrifice. You have to be willing to try different things in order to find what's best for you. Many people don't take chances because they fear rejection or failure. But continuing to do the same things in life will keep bringing you the same results. Nothing ever changes unless you change yourself first. That's where I'm at right now in my life: I can't just keep telling myself that I know what I have to do and not try it. Most people know their issues and what they have to do to change them, but they fear other people's reactions. The only answer to that is to choose the people you feel most comfortable with and ignore everyone else. But in return, you also have to be willing to accept people's ways if you want them to respect your choices.

Understand that it is going to be a lonely feeling when you decide to go a different direction in life. It's tough when you are used to seeing the same people and doing the same things you have been doing since you were a kid and then, all of a sudden, deciding to do things differently. But you have to try to do what's best for you and your life.

Everything else will fall into place. I have spent most of my life trying to satisfy most of my friends and family members. At the time, I thought it was what I was supposed to do. Not to say that I have any regrets, but I wish I would have concentrated more on myself as opposed to trying to make everyone else happier. I used to think that life was mostly about giving, and it turns out that I was right. I believe that most of us go through life trying to satisfy others to gain their acceptance and for fear of being alone or not liked. But you must understand that the only people you should ever take care of are the people that would take care of you in return.

Chapter 14

Living Proof

*F*or those that don't think that life is what you make it, *I'm living proof that-change is always an option*. Many I've come across tell me that all they know how to do is take the easy way out because it is too hard to make it in this world. We all know life is not easy, especially when you're the main reason why it has become hard. The choices you make in life are what make your path in life easier or harder to deal with. Everything that you have or haven't done in life is what makes others decide whether you're worth their time or not. If you continue to choose to do the same shit all your life, why should you ever expect different results? You never get better at doing stupid shit. People are judged by the past and the present, not by the promises they make about the future. And these days, most people are full of shit—they will lie all day just to make it through the night.

I used to turn my issues into bigger problems because I didn't get my way. Now I understand that many things that we go through in life are experiences we need to learn from. If you get to a certain point in your life and end up disappointed with yourself, understand that nobody else is responsible for the choices you've made. It took me many years to figure out that no matter how much I change my ways, it will never change my past. Just because I changed my way of being and thinking didn't necessarily mean that everything or everyone around me will adapt to me either. In life, it's all about who you trust. It's about who will be there for you when you're fucked. But most importantly and above all it's all about what makes you happy.

Seeing is believing. It takes a person facing reality to understand that life is real. You can warn people, you can scare them, and you can even show them examples of the many things that can happen. Unfortunately, in most cases, it's not until it is too late to get out of a situation that a person looks back into his or her life and wonders what it would have been like had he or she taken a different route and made better choices. It doesn't take a genius to figure out where I went wrong. I've been through a lot of shit in my life, but I understand that I chose to go that route. A new pair of sneakers and an edge up was more important to us than getting our shit together. Although I stress a lot about where I stand today, I understand that it could have been a hell of a lot worse. Shit, I'm lucky to still be breathing. There were only two places I pictured myself being when I was asked what I thought I would be doing in five years: doing time or gone and forgotten about.

Everyone's life is different. Life is what you make it, not what others lead you to believe it is. No one in this world should tell you what's best for you. There is nothing wrong with trying new things in life. Nine times out of ten, you should be able to look ahead and see whether a choice you want to make will end up being beneficial to you or a big disappointment. There are going to be many things that you go through in life that you won't be able to change. These are the situations that you will either learn from or suffer constantly from. It's part of growing up. It's a lot easier to live a loser's life because there are so many choices you can make to get what you want without having to struggle, but what's the point of not earning things when it could easily be taken away?

Misery doesn't always need company when you're your worst enemy. Sometimes all it takes is a mirror for you to see the truth; you don't always have to hear it. They say that God has a plan for you, but that doesn't mean that it's just going to fly out of the sky and land on your lap. I say that because I know that when it comes to thinking about God, I'm sure He's not the one who puts these illegal things in your mind for you to go and try. I'm not saying that He's not going to test you at times and put you in some unfortunate situations for you to learn from or deal with, but it's all about how you respond and bounce back that really matters. If you continue to keep making the same mistakes, He wants nothing to do with that. It's just like when you disobey your parents: the disappointment will never hurt more than the consequences. I'm far from religious although I believe that there is something more than what we are dealing with here on earth. But even if there is nothing after all this is over, why would you want to waste it where there's so much to do while you're alive. The fast life isn't going to get you anywhere besides broke, incarcerated, homeless, or killed.

If you are living an unhappy life, you always have the choice to change that. If you decide that you're just going to sit back and complain all your life instead of making changes, what you should do is accept what you have become. Why not be proud of your own accomplishments? Don't accuse or blame anyone else for your own mistakes. It was your dreams that became nightmares. Nobody else should have to suffer from that besides you. By the age of twenty-one, you should have an idea about what it is you want to do with yourself. If you have no idea or goal, you better think fast. The military will sound like a better option when you are desperate than starving under a bridge or stressing in a prison cell.

I never really understood the mentality of people who were constantly going in and out of prison: they become so institutionalized that they think that they are better than the system and never seem to accept the consequences for their own actions. Here's what I tell people who constantly end up on that side of the fence: what you get in return for your act may never seem fair, but how is what you did to the victim any better? Plain and simple, you can't go to hell and tell the devil how to run his place. And by the devil, I don't mean white people. I say that because that's the first thing that comes out of our mouths when we get caught doing something we either knew was illegal or wrong. Now I am not saying that we as minorities are not being profiled or targeted sometimes, but at the same time, hanging out on the streets all day all night makes you a target as it is. You may consider it harassment, but are you doing anything positive or legal while you're hanging out there? Shit, I knew we weren't. We were easy targets for the police to fuck with us at any given time. And as much as I hated them, I have to admit, I was breaking the law 24 hours a day every day for nearly 20 years. I was just mad because they were always interrupting our fun.

I've always hated pressure. I could never stand being questioned. I hated not being able to have control over my own choices and decisions in my life. But you know when that ended? It ended when I decided to begin to do the right things in life. No one should ever have to answer to anyone else other than their parents or their boss. Once you decide to break the rules and laws, you're fucked. Once you are stripped of your freedom, you won't even have control over where you piss or shit. And it sucks that, as an adult, you have to answer to someone else who you may not even know or would have never met had you not fucked up. Why should a grown man or woman have to be told how to live or what to do? You should be at home telling your own kids what to do.

I always wanted to change, even when I was out there fucking up. The only thing I didn't want to do was listen. I used to get tired of hearing others tell me what they thought was right for me. One thing I have learned is that the person who gives you advice does not necessarily have to mean what he or she is saying. Most who give advice usually contradict themselves if they were in the situations they are trying to save you from. But it's not who's saying it that really matters at that time. It's what's being said that is most important. Back in the day, I would listen to a loser before I would listen to my own parents. I used to think that my parents were just telling me what to do because they were being assholes. I didn't realize that what they really wanted was the best things for me and my future. For me, it was like praying to God for something versus doing it the fast way. The devil usually always won because he answered quicker. You just had to be ready and willing to deal with the consequences when they came.

I thank God everyday for where I'm at today. I know that I have said that I have lived a shitty life, but in all honesty, something got me to where I'm at today in one piece. I am very grateful that I don't have to complain or struggle in the same ways that many others I hung out with do today. You can judge me by what I used to be when I was younger; you can point the finger and say that I used to be a fucking *Loser*. But no matter what people think of me, there is nothing they can say about me that I don't already know. My mistakes got me here. And I'm proud of who and where I am. So when anyone says that life is fucked up, I can always say that I agree. But what I can't agree with is a person giving up. If you give up, others will give up on you, too. Life is a like a marathon: if you get tired, people will just keep passing you by.

It doesn't matter where you start. It's where you end up. Believe me; I know from experience that we all go through some if not many unfortunate situation in life.

Some will learn from others and never forget.

But that's life.

Chapter 15

Never Say Never

*W*hy should anyone in this world care more about you than you should about yourself? No one on this earth owes shit. You are and should be responsible for all your acts in life. One thing that I used to always say to myself was that, no matter how anyone tries to scare me about my future, I will never be that *Loser* they always talked about. Although I have failed many times, I always got right back up and kept trying no matter how hard it was to make it past my worries. I was scared as hell and still am about being homeless or dying of hunger. I use it as motivation. Do you know how many people said it wouldn't be them and are now out there struggling, waking up hungry and cold each and every night? Do you think that their goal in life was to be homeless and begging for change?

It all begins by having these dreams of making it the easy way. If you are constantly depending on the same hustle all your life, time will keep passing you by until everything catches up to you. Meanwhile, you're burning bridges with family and acting like you will never need them no matter how much you struggle. Let me talk to you about pain. Have you ever been so hungry that your stomach feels like it's turning into a knot? It's a pain that, that unless you've actually felt it, you will never know it's hard to take. It will have you walking around with your eyes popping out of your head, bent over like a heroin addict. That day that I experienced and spoke about was true: I really did look into a garbage can and stared at a pork chop.

It was around the time when two of my brothers and about fifteen of my friends got locked up after they had been snitched on. Out of all of us, I was the only one that wasn't arrested even though they had also raided my house thinking that I had been hiding drugs there too. That did it or me. I didn't leave the house for weeks. I couldn't go out and try to make money anymore because I thought they were still watching me. I still had a trunk full of drugs that I had just picked up the day before the raid in New York.

There was no food in the house and the cops had taken all of our money. I was left dead broke. Starving one night, as I was tossing something in the garbage, I noticed a pork chop that had been thrown away half eaten the day before. I stared at it for what felt was about five minutes. It was at that moment that I realized I had to change. It was my turning point. The people I have told that story to always looked at me like I was just making it up. But I'm not worried about what they think; I'm more worried about reliving that experience again.

Let me bring you back to 2002 for a minute. That was the year when I finally gave it all up. Once my brothers and all of my friends had gotten snitched on, I felt like the last man standing. Trust and believe that I really went through it. Remember, drug dealing was all I knew how to do since I was 12 years old. But although things had to come to an end for me, I believe that all of these things happened for a really good reason. Most of you will probably read this and either be pissed about it or will entirely disagree with me. But in a crazy way, that snitch probably saved our lives. We had been living recklessly up to that point. There was nothing that we didn't have. We had all the guns we needed, the popularity, and most importantly, we were all making money. But in the end, once every one was released from prison, every one moved on to living better lives.

I try each and every day to escape everything that has kept me from moving forward in life. But in reality, I love the fact that I have struggled. You never know yourself until you are tested by the most difficult situations in life. It's the people who forget their struggles who constantly find themselves repeating the past. Life is no joke, man. You can go from being on top one minute to being so far in a hole that no one hears your cries. I've been there with a shovel in my hand that helped me keep digging deeper and deeper until my life became nothing but darkness with no light in sight. Somehow, I kept reaching up and made it out. And one thing that makes it all special is that it wasn't the people I was always around who helped me get out of that hell, it was me: I used my failures as motivation to keep pushing to become somebody. Not to become famous—not a person everyone knew, and not a person who would laugh at others who faced what I have in my past. No, I wanted to become a person who could always say he struggled and dug himself out from the bottom to stand on his own two feet again.

There aren't many people who can say that. There are people out there who get comfortable with their failures and give up. They sign up for all kinds of help and forget what life was all about. They forget how much better it felt to work hard to earn things in life instead of expecting handouts. I don't know why, but it pisses me off like nothing else when I see a grown man who is still walking and talking perfectly just sitting back collecting because he is lazy. One day, I saw this guy who looked healthy enough to get a job begging for change in front of a liquor store. He asked me for change so I gave him advice. He told me that he understood everything that I said but that all he needed was change. I told him I just tried, and he looked at me like I was stupid. Since he didn't understand what I was trying to say, I told him that I would bring him back an application to help him change. He looked at me, got pissed off, and walked away. Help comes in many forms in life. It's completely up to you to accept the help or turn it down.

The point that I am making is that, once people settle in their ways, they don't want to go back to find out where they got lost. They just keep going down this long highway, lost and ignoring all the exits they could have taken. In all honesty, I don't care what anyone says: you can stop what you're doing and change. People just choose not to do so. For every choice you want to make, there are many examples right in front of you that should help you make the right ones. You see them under bridges, you see them being kicked out of the way of business doors, you see them in front of stores asking for change, and you see them lined up begging for free food or diving in a dumpster. And I feel sorry for the situation that they are in, but I always wonder why they never try to get back on their feet and try hard to get out of the struggle that they are in.

What would you rather do? Work a good job and get paid or do community service? Use your social security number on an application or continue to yell out your prison number? Have freedom and the liberties or be treated like a child? Have friends or cellmates? Listen to advice from friends and family or have a parole officer telling you what to do? Be homeless or living with family? Graduate from school or work minimum wage? Change your ways on your own or be forced to? I'm not just talking shit; I had to make these changes myself. These are the things that I had to go through to understand that, when it comes to the life of a *Loser*, these are the things that I would eventually be facing in my life. Thankfully, I made the right choices. I changed at the right time. It took me a while to understand what was more important, but I made it out. Mentally, I still fuck up sometimes because I react in ways that I know I shouldn't. But physically, I will never place myself in a position where it will be up to another adult to correct my decisions.

That's all part of growing up. It's part of being an adult. You can't continue to go the rest of your life bitching and complaining. Life is like a building: it must be built one brick at a time. You have to start from the bottom and work your way up. You fuck up one too many times and everything will come tumbling down. Nobody in life can say that they haven't had some type of help or heard some advice that they could have listened to. If you choose to reject everything and everyone trying to help you, you better hope that your plans in life work for you. And if you're one of those people who really don't care and always want to take the easy way out, it doesn't get easier than being locked up and not having to worry about the everyday struggles. That may be what you need. Just know and always keep in mind that one wrong decision in your life can have you spending the rest of it in regret.

You have to stop and think about what it is that you want out of your life. If you make the choice to continue going down the wrong paths in life, you can't expect anyone to continue feeling sorry for you. Regardless of how hard life gets, you have to understand that this life is all you have. What's life without living it freely and being happy? Everyone in this world who has made it to becoming what they always wanted to be in life has struggled somehow. No one in this world just wakes up one day and is given what they want. Even those who are rich and have everything they always wanted struggled in life somehow. That's what life is all about. Not everything in this world or in your life is going to be easy. And the harder you make it, the worse it becomes. Today's issues are practice to make everything else easier for tomorrow. Until then, make the right choice, live in peace, or rest in it.

Chapter 16

Death before Dishonor

*I*n this day and age, there are hardly any people you can actually trust. There is not a secret in this world that a person can't wait to spread. They say that promises are meant to be broken. But what's a secret if two people know? A lot of people have loose lips these days. People talk faster than they think, not knowing that they are spreading business that they shouldn't. But how can you really control that? The one and only way is to keep what you never want spread to yourself. I don't ever tell anyone anything that I don't want repeated to others. If I say it to one person, I wouldn't care if I were questioned about it from others. Like the saying goes, ask me no questions and I'll tell you no lies. In the streets, it's the complete opposite: it all depends on the situation.

These are the reasons why I never had that many friends. But most importantly, although I understand the bonds that gang members and drug dealers think they have amongst each other, when the shit hits the fan, everyone is at risk of being snitched on. By the time you end up in handcuffs, you'll definitely be shocked to find out that it is usually the ones you told everything to who put you under. It happens every time. It's easy to believe each other when there are no consequences in hand. As soon as a person notices that he or she is going to be facing prison time, they're ready to snitch before they even step one foot in the courtroom. Believe me when I tell you that I have barely ever come around that many people who have kept their word. I'm not necessarily just talking about snitching to the authorities. I'm talking about people who run their mouths all day about things they were trusted with. Some people talk and don't even realize that they are pretty much just handing over the missing piece to someone else's puzzle.

What's sad is that people these days trust the words of a person making all kinds of promises and living a fake dream rather than listening to someone who has already dealt with some kind of consequence similar to what they may be facing. When they say that the truth shall set you free, they must have been talking about those who tell. *Because as soon as they face incarceration, they're walking right out of the police department fearing nothing.* When you're facing time, you realize that most if not everything you ever did to get to that point was definitely never worth it. Think about this for a minute. What would you do if they were trying to sentence you to life in prison and you didn't even commit the crime? Are you going to spend the rest of your life in prison because you gave someone your word? Do you think they anyone else would do the same for you? That's how you'll find out how *real* these people are. You'll likely notice that a person's word never meant shit from the moment you first shook hands.

The more people you hang around, the more mouths there are to tell the story. Most will give you their word before they give you their back. They give you their word because they want be part of something. But are they going to continue being loyal once they face consequences on their own? Will they take your place in a courtroom or will they point the finger at you from the witness stand?

It's a double-edged sword: if you tell, you might be free, but if they know you told, some might try to kill you. So why even get down? If you know deep in your heart that there may be a chance that the people you surround yourself with may turn their backs on you, why would you even take the risk? And snitching on you is incredibly easy. They might even be the ones to have you set up ... or even kill you themselves.

Look at the history of gangs. They all start out with a plan. And then you end up with a few ignorant ones who fuck up everything. You start out with a little crew trying to have fun, but before you know it, you're downtown facing life in prison. Snitches are a cop's best friend. Have you not noticed that cops don't ride around wasting gas anymore looking for criminals? All they do now is sit back and wait for information. And guess who's doing all the telling? Criminals just like you who fear going to prison. I'll be honest; there are many people who hang out in the streets who have no other intentions than making money. Not everyone is built to do prison time. But if you're not smart enough to figure those people out and settle with them just because they shake your hand and share a few laughs, don't ever be surprised if you get told on. It's hard to deal with it, but it is much harder to accept that the ones you always trust are the ones who know everything about you and tell.

Before I give you my word, I would rather not give you my time. I'm not going to spend all my time in one place. I don't have enough time to be doing time. Because I have to be honest, my life comes first before anybody else's. I'm not talking shit about those who choose to lose their lives for others over colors or because they are boys. If that's what you choose to do with your life, I wish you all the luck in the world. If you can handle doing time for other people's crimes instead of being there for your real family, be real to yourself. If your reason for joining a gang is because you never had a real family, you may never get the chance to make your own after you choose others in place of that choice.

If good things come to those who wait, I would guess that bad things happen to those who rush. The only thing you can trust these days are the things that are in black and white: a statement and a warrant. The fewer people you hang out with, the fewer places you will go, and the fewer risks you will take. Everyone in this world has an angle. Most people have plans that may not coincide with yours. Guilty by association can easily be turned into a guilty verdict. A judge isn't going to lie to you, and neither will the jury when it puts you away forever. They won't turn their backs on you. They will tell you the truth and nothing but the truth when you beg God to help you. I guess you should be happy about one thing: you wore a suit to court instead of wearing it in a coffin.

Chapter 17

Can't Go Back

One thing that most street hustlers and criminals have in common is always pushing aside the good people and things they have in their lives. They push aside their families, they no longer want to hang out with their childhood friends, and they spend little (if any) time with the people they claimed to love. I was guilty of all three. These are the three situations that will leave a person going crazy in a cell. When they hang out on the streets, none of these people are important to them. When they end up in a cell, they are the ones they quickly try to reach out to. I used to hang out on the streets. I know what it is like to shit on the people you should love and cherish the most. Although I never ended up doing prison time, I always knew that, if I did, these people I left behind were going to talk the most shit about me if I tried to reach out to them.

So I never burned bridges with family like most of the idiots I hung around with did. I always knew family and friends were important.

The streets were always a priority for me, just like they are for a lot of people out there today. They can see their boys get locked up and shot or killed every day and still continue doing their thing. But it's not until someone really close to them dies that their lives will probably change. It's like me: from one day to the next, I viewed life from a whole new perspective, but it wasn't like I just sat there and said to myself that I had to change. There are things in life that don't give you that choice. When these things happen to you unexpectedly, those last minutes will be relived every day until you find closure. Closure is something that has no time limit. It will take some a few months and others about a year or two. As for me, I don't think I'll ever get past it because till this day, the murder of one of my closest friends still plays in my thoughts as if it occurred yesterday.

And I know that no matter how many times I tell people, each and every one of them will tell me that it was meant to be or that it was just his time. I try to agree with some of it. These are life situations that, unless you live through, you'll never fully understand. What's difficult about life is that it always takes the worst for us to wake up and understand what was in front of us. We never expect tragedy. We never think that the people who are in front of us may not be there tomorrow. Shit, you might not be here tomorrow. I wish I could wake up one day and say that this was all just a crazy nightmare, but I know that it's not. There are many people out there who are constantly doing the same things I went through before I learned through my own tragic experience. But they won't see or understand what I'm trying to say until it happens to them.

I see people go in and out of prison every day—kids arguing with and cursing out their family members like they don't mean shit to them. But I lost someone who I really looked up to. You have the opportunity to see, feel, and talk to the people you should treat better. Why would you want to continue going down a path that's only going to take you through hell? You don't have to listen to me. You'll never feel what I feel or have dealt with until you have to end up dealing with your own mistakes and consequences. I don't care how tough you are; I don't care how much money you make; I couldn't care less about you being a thug or being institutionalized. Keep on fucking up and one day you will experience for yourself what I'm saying.

Life is not a joke. Stop wasting your life on bullshit. *The streets ain't shit.* I wish I could go back to many different situations and handle them differently. Even though I take all of the things I've been through as life's experiences, the rough shit still hurts. If you choose to continue fucking up, all of these things I have written about will eventually land you right where I stand today. Regretting your past and wishing you could start all over again. You still have a chance. Your family, your close ones, and those real friends aren't going to be there forever. Don't be like me and treat the ones who really love and care about you poorly. Stop expecting that they are going to be there for you no matter how you treat them. They might not even be there for you to apologize for the way you have treated them.

And believe me, that part will hurt us the most.

People hurt every day. But when you have to deal with it alone, it's a completely different experience.

In Closing

Repeated History

There's a tug of war in life between right and wrong that results in two things: life and death. People in this world seem to be very confused about the difference between choices and the decisions about mistakes and accidents. Many people play with their lives daily until the worst happens to them. It is unfortunate that the worst things have to occur for people to open their eyes to the reality and the dangers of crime. As long as there are human beings in this world, there are always going to be opinions. Unfortunately, the facts don't get through to people until it is already too late. Remember, people in this world are judged by their past, not by what they promise to others they will do in the future. The streets and the criminal lifestyles that people choose—yes, choose—have been claiming the lives of many good people. Not every criminal is bad; they are loved by their friends and family members. But one thing that we have to begin to open up our eyes about is that every victim in the streets could have easily been the prime suspect of the crimes they are taken out by. Every victim in the streets may have also been the suspect to the many crimes no one has been apprehended for. Those who don't know how dangerous the streets really are need to pay close attention to all of the things that have been occurring not only in their city, but also around the world. Everyone in the streets will have an enemy at one point or another. They will also have an encounter that may result in a life-and-death situation.

We can blame the police, we can blame the government, we can blame society, we can blame our parents, and we can blame the environment we live in. But in reality, these issues should be blamed on the individuals who choose particular paths. People make choices based on what they feel comfortable with doing in their own lives. Some choose to live the street life because of boredom, whereas many others choose the streets because they claim that is all they know. Unfortunately, most people never give other things a chance because they are impatient with the slow results of living a positive life. At a young age, there are not too many who are willing to adapt to the patience that it takes to be successful. Everyone wants the quick pay and the quick results. But where does that bring you? Have you ever tried taking a shortcut and ended up getting lost more than you were when you first started? So many young people these days choose the wrong paths simply because they can't see the danger that awaits them on the other side. They expect to get away with the same things they got away with yesterday and continue to take the same risks.

One thing that I learned in life at an early age was that every leader was also a follower at one point in their lives. They had to learn the ins and outs of the life they chose in order to get to where they were. Unfortunately, no one will ever lead their followers to pass them in the chain of command. So once a follower sees that there is no way up the ladder, they go their separate ways and form their own things. This is how violence spreads. Everyone is constantly looking for a way in and some success. But while trying to get these things, they will constantly come across many others who want the same things. In reality, there is no end to these issues in sight. Matters will only continue to get worse and worse. There really is no cure for negativity besides prison or death—unless the individual wants to change.

These young kids who choose the streets as a way of life don't listen to others who have been through it in their past. What would make anyone think that they should listen to a teacher in a classroom or a probation or parole officer for a short period of time? Look at everyone who has been through the street life and what they say about it. Most, if not all, will tell you that it was never worth going through. Look at all those people who are locked up for years, if not life, and they will say the same thing. Kids these days only listen to the ones they stand next to each and every day. Advice is boring to them. They don't want to hear about what's good for them; they don't have that vision to look into the future. Often, prison makes matters even worse. Because now they will be judged by their criminal records and no one is willing to give them an opportunity to prove themselves. This is really sad to say, but the only thing that will help each and every individual who chooses the street life is to go through it and get out on their own. There is a small percentage of individuals who may be saved, but compared to those numbers, there are far too many no one will ever reach.

The problem only doubles when most of these teens become adults and never change their way of living. All this does is keep the cycle going. These adults who never changed may end up having kids who end up just like them, or worse. It sucks to say, but a prison may be a lot safer than the streets these days. This is where most of these kids will end up because they concentrate more on their reputation then they do on their lives. One of the many ways I could have chosen to better myself and my life was to find a routine. If most of these kids found a job or played sports it would limit the risk of being shot, killed, or locked up. But hanging out in the streets as if it were a place of employment will eventually get you terminated one way or another.

In the streets, they say that only the lucky ones make it out. On the other side of that, the good ones die. If you put those two together, the percentage of the ones who dodge death or life in prison forever by changing their ways is very small. It's very hard to let go of a lifestyle you wake up to everyday. But you will always find out just how close you and your friends really were when you try to make a difference for the better. As for me, I've learned to stop feeling sorry for those who continue to struggle and suffer in life by choice. I know how hard it is to change, but I know from my own experiences that it is possible. It's a lot easier said than done; it takes a lot of patience and dedication—but in the end, it is worth it. Unfortunately, most won't take that route due to their ego and pride.

There is a rap song by The Notorious Big that says *"You're Nobody"* (Till Somebody Kills You). In most cases, I would say that it shouldn't be that way. But when it comes to the streets, it is not too far from the truth. I wonder how many people would have cared about me had I been killed in the streets. Initially, people would have forgotten all of the wrong things I ever did when they spoke about me at my wake. I probably would have been made out to be an angel in fear that someone would retaliate for speaking bad about me as I laid in a coffin. Maybe someone would have tattooed my name on their arm. It is unfortunate, but when we are alive, we all seem to be taken for granted.

Once we are no longer here, everyone claims they loved us and miss us.

Don't just be a statistic.

9 781545 636305